The Pink Room

Heather Maggio

 pencil

ISBN 978-93-5667-363-2
© Heather Maggio 2023
Published in India 2023 by Pencil

A brand of
One Point Six Technologies Pvt. Ltd.
123, Building J2, Shram Seva Premises,
Wadala Truck Terminal, Wadala (E)
Mumbai 400037, Maharashtra, INDIA
E connect@thepencilapp.com
W www.thepencilapp.com

Author biography

My name is Heather Maggio, I am a mother of four beautiful, amazing chidren. Three boys and one girl. I also have five precious grandchildren. I have three girls and two boys. They absolutely make my world go round. My life wasnt the easiest, but I wouldnt trade it for the world. I lost my husband, best friend, and love of my life in 2015. He was diagnosed with stage 4 colon in 2012 and three short years, he lost the battle with that horrible disease. I thought I would never be able to go on, but found the strength through Jesus Christ, my personal Saviour. I was raised in a Christian home with an amazing stepdad and my mom. My biological father left us when I was young, and you can read all about that in my book From a Widow to a Warrior, also here in Pencil app. You will read how my journey to come to know the Lord, was not as easy as you would have thought, if you knew my parents. I thank God they stayed on their knees praying for me, because without that, Im so afaid to even think of where I may have wound up. But I truly would not change one thing because it was the trials and every situation or circumstance that brought me to this point. I could have never in a million years dreamed that I would have written two books, it just was never anything that interested me. I would laugh and joke with friends and say "I could write several books, with everything I have been through". And we just laughed, but never imagined that dream would actually become reality. I hope you enjoy this book as much as I enjoyed writing it.

CONTENTS

Acknowledgements

This book is dedicated to my Mama...because she stayed on her knees praying for me alongside my stepdad. I can't even begin to tell you what they mean to me. My Mama is the strongest woman I know, and lived a Christian life and was the closest thing to an angel. I'm blessed to be her daughter. I love you to the moon and back again, Mom

Introduction

This book is about a place that I never dreamed I would find myself. I had never been to jail in my life. But there I was in my mid 40's in jail. How did I get there? Well, it all started a normal day, until my husband at the time decided he wanted to have a friend over but that wasnt where the problem was. Once he got him there, he decided he wanted to go get high. Yep, he had just gotten out of a three month rehab program, but there he was walking in the door his friend standing there and he had gone and gotten high. I couldnt believe it, but that is not where it gets good. He then decided he wanted to put his hands on me and hit me, as if I was a man, not his wife. His parents got wind of this, called the cops and it went straight down hill from there. He would wind up going to jail, me left there with this friend of his I had just met. So i took it upon myself to drive his friend home, since my husband had gotten put in jail, I surely did not want to be there at my own house with a complete stranger to me. That would turn into the worst day of my life. Truly my life was about to take a turn for the worst. But it actually wound up being the day that changed my life forever.

NOW WHAT...

The pink room was the worst smelling, filthy, cold, little, place you could ever imagine. But I will so my best to explain it to you. It all started when the officer brought me into "D" block. I remember walking in and thinking to myself "Im going to just die here". The guard stripped me down and gave me an orange pair of paints that were about four sizes too big, and an orange shirt that was also about four sizes too big. She gave me a pair of orange flip flops that were probably about two sizes too big and told me to have a seat and wait there and she woud be back to put me in my cell later. So I sat down on this hard metal bench that was attached to this table and painted pink. The gate that led down the hall where the other inmates were was locked so I could not see anyone, I could only hear them. So i sat there a while in disbelief this was happening again, only this time I knew I had done nothing wrong. The guard finally came in and brought me to my cell. There were two other females in there already, so I layed my mat on the floor and layed down on it. I spoke to them and they spoke to me, but that was about it. Later that night we started talking and telling each other our stories. I remember one of the girls told me she was in there for attempted murder. She went on to tell me about her stepdad, and how he tried to molest her all her life, and she finally had enough one day and tried to kill him. I thought to myself how lucky I was to have had such a wonderful Christian mom and stepdad that raised me. We talked a while, cried a while, and then the other girl started telling me about her life and how she wound up in there. Her story was quite intersting too, but on a different level. She began by telling me how her boyfriend was very abusive to her, even tried killing her. But she said how much she loved him!! I though"WOW" how is this even possible? But that was all she knew. They even lived in the woods behind her dads house. She talked about the night he would beat her up and accuse her of cheating on her, all the while, she had never left his side. But hey were also doing drugs together. So that played a huge roll in the lifestyle she chose to live. But she was trying to get her life back together and get her kids back.They were living with her siter. She was trying to get into the drug court program. So we talked about that and what her plans were when she got out, and how she just wanted to have a normal life with her kids. I sat there and listened to these young ladies tell their stories, and I thought about my ilfe. I had not been living the "perfect" life, but somehow my problems and issues just were not so big anymore, and I realized then what a truly good life I had growing up. I thanked God for that, and I thanked God that I never had to go down these roads before. I can tell you that even as bad as you think your problems are and sometimes they are, if you just sit and listen to someone elses story, the situaiton you may be going through at the moment doesnt seem so bad after all. We continued to talk to each other and consoled each other and then decided we woud lay down and try to get some sleep befoe the guards came in and we got in trouble, because the lights had been turned off for about an hour by this time. So we layed down and went to sleep.

Where are the clocks...

Time passed so slow. they would make us sit in our cells that were 6x8, which was not very big when you had three to four ladies in a cell at one time. These cells were so small you could barely move around in them. They had a bunkbed welded to the wall, and painted pink. , A metal toilet and a sink attached to it, that was the only thing that wasnt painted pink. Every morning, the guards would come in at 5:00am to bring breakfast. The breakfast was the same every single morning For breakfast we would have one sausage patty, and two tortillas. These torillas were not the normal size tortillas you have at home or get in the grocery store. These torillas were the same size as he sausage patty. We also would get oatmeal or grits, but most days oatmeal, and either an apple or an orange, most days an apple. You wouldnt normally eat your fruit, because you learned quickly you would want something later on, and so most of the ladies wouldl save their fruit. After trays were passed to each inmate, they would come back in with a cooler on a rolling cart, and inside was powdered milk. They would pass in front of every cell and ask if you wanted milk, and if you did you would hand them your cup, If you had one and they would put your milk in it. After breakfast trays were picked up, one of the guards would comein and tell us to stand by the wall. This happened usually around 7:00 am. Your bed had to be made neatly, and your cell clean by this time. The guard would come in and the cell doors would open for us to stand against the wall in the hallway. Then the guards would go into each cell and inspect each one. They were checking for things that were not supposed to be in there. One time they found orange peels in one of the girls shampoo bottle, They would put orange peels in their shampoo to give their hair moisture. When the guard found the shampoo bottle with the orange peels in it, she told the inmate that she needed to throw it away, because if she didnt she was going to get a contraband charge. So the girl threw her bottle of shampoo away. Then after all the cells were checked we were told to go back in and the cell doors would lock behind us. Then around 10:30 am it would be time for lunch. This was the main meal of the day. Every week we would be served the best thing. Mondays we would have chicken pattys, green beans, and a spoonful of lettuce with no dressing. The same ice chest that they served powdered milk for breakfat would have juice, if you were lucky and if not you just got some luke warm water, Tuesdays we had pork and beans over rice, corn, and a handful of lettuce again, no dressing. Wednesdays we would have chicken fried steak, green beans, and cornbread. Thursday was Lima beans over rice and mixed vegetables with cornbread. Fridays was tacos or hamburgers. Weekends were never the same but you could almost bet it would be beans and something mixed in with it. But time seemed to drag on and on. We only knew about what time it was by the meals we were brought.

The girl in cell seven....

At the end of the hall was cell seven, and inside that cell was a girl we never saw. Her lights didn't work and they didn't bother to change the bulbs. We would hear her sing sometimes, curse the guards, and even threw food at them through the bars of her cell. The door to her cell never opened, and nobody even talked about her. It's like a mystery to this day, but when I asked one of the guards about her they would just say "Were trying to find a place to put her!"and left it at that. So I left it alone. One day we smelled something and knew it was her because she never came out to take a shower, her cell door was never opened the entire three months I was there. So we asked the guards could they please give her a shower because the smell was getting to be unbearable. So they did alright, they brought a fire hose in, just like the ones used by firefighters and sprayed her down with that hose, cell doors remained closed. But everyone was too afraid, or just knew better than to say something.

One Thursday, early afternoon, the guards came in and told us we would not be getting out if our cells "till further notice" as per the wardon. We asked why and all they said was "they didn't have any idea why, that was all the wardon told them". So again we sat in our small cells behind the bars for four days and the following Monday, we were able to get our normal 1 hour to go into the dayroom to watch tv. But the girl in cell seven stayed in her cell as usual. I never did find out who she was or what she had done. But when i left she was still there in cell seven.

Showers please....

Showers are a luxury!!!! Yes what we take for granted are luxuries at this place. Now let me be clear. I do not think a jail should be a place that is luxurious, but humane is not asking to much either. I do believe all jails should have running water, and not showers that don't drain, mold everywhere you look, and a button you have to keep pressing like the water fountains at schools to get the water to trickle out of. Well what I just explained ws the shower we had to use. Only when the guards that were working "allowed" us to take showers. It was in the dayroom where we watched tv with a shower curtain that closed. A small stall with a shower head and a button on the wall to press to get water out. No hot water, sometimes Luke warm but never hot. There was one button that controlled the water, and the water dud nit drain do we had to put a milk crate in there to stand on so you wouldn't have water up to your knees because of the drainage issues. But honestly it felt good just to get halfway clean.

Mondays were the days we would get our state supplies and these supplies were supposed to last us the whole week. State supplies were one roll of toilet paper, bar of soap, small botle of shampoo, and small tube of toothpaste. We got these on Monday and it was supposed to last all week. Then the next thing we knew, we stopped getting those supplies. The first couple of weeks weren't bad because if we needed something most times someone else had extra and would share. Then those that had stocked up started running out of things and the next thing we knew nobody had any toilet paper, soap, etc etc not even saved or put up. We would ask the guards for toilet paper and they claimed they didn't have any, we were totally dumbfounded. Had no idea what we would do, so we had no choice but to use socks as toilet paper. After a month with no state supplies being passed out we finally were told they had some for us. So they came in and brought us a roll of toilet paper and half of annar of soap. The had taken the bars of dial soap and Irish spring and cut them I'm half so we each had half a bar. We were just grateful for the half bar of soap and roll of toilet paper. Things could not have gotten any worse, literally.

Wait, what...

Time continues to drag on and on in the pink room, and i still didn't have a date that I was going to get out, only an estimate. It was January, and cold inside those concrete walls. I remember freezing what felt like to death. But I was at peace because i had been soul searching, reading the Bible, and soul searching. It was the longest three months of my life, but I believe in my heart it was probably the best thing to happen to me. I accepted Jesus as m personal Savior and really took the time I was there reading my Bible and thanking God for saving my life.

I was so cold, so I asked the guard if she would please look in my personal items for a long sleeve shirt I had on when I got there, and she agreed to look for me. A few hours passed and she finally came back in, but no shirt. So I asked her if she found it, and she said "I didn't look, but I need you to sign these papers for me!" I immediately thought what is this and what could this be that she wants me to sign? I said "No disrespect, but I don't want to sign anything, and I hope you understand why!". She responded by saying "I think you will want to sign this!!" So I took the papers and immediately started crying!!!! They had calculated my time and it was time for me to go home!!!! TIME SERVED!!!!! I was so excited, I almost didn't even believe her, but she smiled and said, "Your time is up"!!!! All I could do was run to my cell and get my things and I hit my knees and started thanking God again. So I was released!! I walked out of that jail with my garbage bag full of my personal items and no shoes, (they couldn't find the shoes I had on when I was brought to jail) but that didn't stop me. I walked to the end of the road and stopped at a bailbonds office to wait for my ride that was on its way from where I was from.

Life after the pink room....

That's not where my story ends. God never said it would be easy, BUT what he did say is "I will never leave you or forsake you". And He didn't. So after I got out of jail, I didn't have a car, place to live, etc etc . As you know the landlord, and finance companies didnt wait for me to get my life back in order, so I lived with a "friend" or so I thought. But this person turned out not to be what I call a friend. He told me to stay with him and we agreed we would half the bills, so I moved in and began trying to get my life in order financially. I got a job and was blessed enough to have one of my friends pick me up for work and bring me home. I had my own room, separate from his, but once I moved in, he assumed I "belonged" to him. Which was not the case. In fact, probably the farthest from the truth than one could imagine. But when I told him that wasn't the agreement and I wasn't interested in him that way, this guy turned into something I was terrified of. As a matter of fact, he reminded me of my biological dad, the one that had me and my mom locked in the bedroom with him as he threatened my pregnant mom. The same man that I remember screaming and yelling at my Mama all those years before.

Yes, the guy I was "roommates" with would hit me, blacked eyes, bruises, the whole nine yards, but I couldn't go anywhere because this was where I lived, and had no other place to go and he knew that. So I stayed there, worked, and paid as much as I could, when all the while he had not been paying his portion. So you guessed it, after 1 1/2 years of living in a trailer with what was supposed to be a friend just helping me get back on track, we were evicted. I thought this is not happening!!!!! Really ? Yes, I had friends, but they all had family's of their own and I wasn't going to impose on anyone, because after all I had brought this all on myself. The difference now was I had truly accepted Jesus as my personal Saviour, and believe you me, if I wouldn't have had Him as my personal Saviour, I don't know how I could have made it out alive, or went through what I went through.

The first year I was out of jail, things weren't a whole lot better, but the difference was I didn't live behind a locked set of bars. I was mentally and physically abused by this so called friend of mine that was supposed to be helping me till I could get back on my feet. I'm still not sure what this person's problem was and probably will never know. But I do know every night I would pray for him because that's what the Bible tells is to do. I'm not saying it was the easiest thing to do, because it wasn't, but I also knew if I didn't pray for him I wasn't doing what I was supposed to do either. I can't tell you how, but I can tell you the only thing I did have was faith. Faith that one day I would be able to go home to a place that was mine and be able to just breathe. By myself...just breathe. But I knew it would probably get worse before it got better. And it did.

So after being evicted his mom told us we could stay at her house and she had a camper inher yard I would be able to stay in if I paid her $120.00 for my part of electricity and water. I agreed and moved into this tiny camper, but it was warm and a roof over my head. I couldn't use the shower in it so I had to go to her house and take my showers and the other problem was I still had no car, and she lived 45 minutes one way to town. So my ride to work couldn't pick me up anymore. So I asked if I payed their gas would her or her husband be able to bring me to work and pick me back up. They agreed but after I got my first check andd payed their gas I didn't even have enough left to pay my rent which was $120.00. So it really did me no good to work, since I paid more in gas than I made.

Not today Satan.....

I thought I was just doomed, but I also knew I had God on my side, and I refused to let Satan take one more thing from me. I was not going to let him steal my joy I had in Jesus. Was it easy? No No No!!!! It was hard, but I never lost faith, because I knew how far I had come. In the meantime, I had been taking online classes to get my degree for a couple of years and only had two years left, so I stayed busy but this place I had moved to after being evicted was like no other place I had been. So, I'll tell you about some of my time spent there in the tiny camper in the yard of the person that had been mentally and physically abusive to me. The people were different out there. Most were very nice, but not the norm I had been raised by. His stepdad was probably the nicest person I met and treated me with respect and tried to help as much as he could. This man could not read or write, but had a kind heart. He was taking care of his mother that had dimentia, and his brother that was blind, but lived in the trailer next toy camper with their mom. I actually got close to him because he taught me things and basically showed me how to do things and especially when you don't have much money. He was a wise man, even though he couldn't read or write. But my friends mother was as mean as her son was. I knew then he had been raised with violence and that was his normal.

About a week after moving out there his mom that had been suffering with dimentia passed away, and his blind brother had never been alone and especially without their mom. So when their mother passed away, he got very depressed. He never came outside, just stayed in the trailer that was next to my camper. One night I remember very well. I was working on a paper that was due for school, when I heard a gunshot. I was scared to death!!! Too scared to even go outside because I had no idea where it had come from. A few minutes later I had a knock on my door. I asked "Who is it?" and his stepdad rellied "Its just me" so I opened the door. He came in to make sure I was ok and told me his brother had shot the gun, but everything was ok, he just was checking on me. I thought, your brother is BLIND, what is he doing with a gun. So of course, if I think it, I say it!!! I said, "but your brother is blind", he kind of laughed and we started talking about something else. I still never found out why, but that was something I never understood.

Meanwhile.....

Oh, the stories I could tell!! But, I want to tell you about my time in "the camper". It was a time I won't soon forget! This place was literally in the middle of NOWHERE!! There were sounds I heard at night, that noone could explain, and I wasn't about to even try, but I'll just say, it was pretty scary ... And rumor was it had been an Indian burial ground, which was true. As a matter not fact, there was one about 50 ft from the front door of the camper, so that is still a mystery to me. But I sure wasn't about to go outside to look, so it will remain a mystery. But I would read my Bible, and work on schoolwork.

The people out there were just different, something I had never seen before. They raised chickens, which wasnt strange to me, but they didn't "go to town" very often, and only socialized with each other. Basically, imagine your next door neighbor being at your house everyday and for Thanksgiving and Christmas that's who you spent it with whether they were related by blood, or related because they lived "on the same hill" as you for the last 10-15 years. So, I felt like an "outsider" intruding on their day to day life l, that was "normal" to them, but not something I was used to. So you I tried to just stay in the camper most of the time, or as much and as long as I could stand without going crazy!!!

They were nice and cordial to me, but it was just awkward. The nicest one was his stepdad. He knew I was trying to just survive and I would always ask if I could help with anything when I would see him out in the yard. But he was very nice to me and tried his best to make me feel more at home. He couldn't read or write, but he was handy and knew how to do most anything. He was also taking care of his mother with dementia and younger brother that lived with their mom. His brother was blind, and on dialysis 3 times a week. About a week after I had moved out there, his mom passed away. I felt so bad for him, but from what he said, *she had been hit too many times in the head" by their father years ago. His dad had already passed a few years before, and I never knew him. But when his mom passed away, it was a sad day.

His younger brother had never lived alone or been without his mom, so he took it really hard. He was blind, so I can imagine how hard it must have been for him too. But I would pray every night for them. This one particular night, I was in the camper, doing schoolwork, and I heard a gunshot and it scared me half to death. I was already pretty uneasy, but it was close, wherever it came from. The next thing I knew, there was a knock on the door, so I asked "who is it?" And it was his stepdad saying, "it's just me", so I got up and opened the door. He was making sure I was ok, and told me his brother had shot the gun outside and he was making sure I was ok. I said I thought he was blind, and he said "he is" I just kind of looked at him and we started talking about something else.

The next day was just another day. But this guy's mom was as mean as he was. They would fuss and argue and say some of the meanest things to each other, and then acted as if nothing was wrong. I was so scared most of the time that I would find myself on the streets because you never knew what or when something was going to go from bad to worse. But I knew then, he had been raised with violence and disfunctuon, so fighting and cursing was his normal. But I just kept to myself and stayed in the Word.

Frustrated, hurt, and bitter....

As I read the Bible, I remember feeling the same feelings Hagar felt, frustrated, hurt, bitter and scared. Hagar knew for a fact, God saw her and God loved her. Hagar had her faults and had also been abused, but God looked past all of that, and saw her future. God knew she would have a son, and he would father a great nation, because she trusted Him. God asked Hagar to do five things; bear a child, be a part of a bad plan that He would turn into a blessing, return to an abusive situation,and lastly she sound expose herself to rejection again. But God also told her to trust Him. When Gid met with her the second time, he asked her to be "apicture of slavery to the Law,", whuch would be essential to everyone in need to reject "futile ways" and draw closer to God.

After Sarah had her own child, she became jealous and asked Abraham to send Hagar and her son away into the wilderness. Hagar must have felt like I felt, scared and alone. Lost in the wilderness and out of water but she cried out to God and wept. God used Hagar and her son, Ishmael and his future wives descendants and formed a great nation, and made 12 tribes. God used them all in such a unique wat, it made me think of our lives as a blank canvas before an artist starts his/her masterpiece

Blank Canvas...

I remember crying out to God, asking "Why, Why, Why?" Then I looked at my life as that blank canvas, and I had brought it all on myself, and this was something that I had to go through, and I was one if the colors in God's masterpiece. So, I embraced everything I was going through and thanked God for saving my lost soul. God cherishes each one of us and it made me smile because I know I will spend eternity with Him in heaven. God is painting a picture of promise that I stand on and it gives me strength to keep going. I know for s fact that even at my lonliest, worst times of my life He remained true to the promises He has given to everyone that has accepted Him as their Lord and Savior. We will always have truaks and obstacles we have to overcome, but I can tell you without a doubt in my mind, if i had not accepted Jesus as my personal Saviour in that small, cold pink, jail cell, I probably would not be here today to tell my story. My prayer for you is that each person that reads this book no matter what your going through, if you trust God and take a step in faith and ask Jesus into your life to be your personal Saviour, your life will never be the same it will not be easy, and you will still have life that is going to continue to knock you down from time to time, but when you have Jesus in your life and accept Him in your heart and truly mean it....your life will change and then you can stand on the promise He gives, and you will spend eternity in heaven with Him...